BOA
EDITIONS LTD

The Day's Last Light Reddens the Leaves of the Copper Beech

T0163985

BOA wishes to acknowledge the generosity of the following
40 for 40 Major Gift Donors

Lannan Foundation
Gouvernet Arts Fund
Angela Bonazinga & Catherine Lewis
Boo Poulin

POETRY BY STEPHEN DOBYNS

The Day's Last Light Reddens the Leaves of the Copper Beech   (2016)
Winter's Journey   (2010)
Mystery, So Long   (2005)
The Porcupine's Kisses   (2002)
Pallbearers Envying the One Who Rides   (1999)
Common Carnage   (1996)
Velocities: New and Selected Poems 1966–1992   (1994)
Body Traffic   (1990)
Cemetery Nights   (1987)
Black Dog, Red Dog   (1984)
The Balthus Poems   (1982)
Heat Death   (1980)
Griffon   (1976)
Concurring Beasts   (1972)

The Day's Last Light Reddens the Leaves of the Copper Beech

POEMS BY

Stephen Dobyns

AMERICAN POETS CONTINUUM SERIES, NO. 156

BOA Editions, Ltd. ❖ Rochester, NY ❖ 2016

Copyright © 2016 by Stephen Dobyns
All rights reserved

First Edition
16 17 18 19 7 6 5 4 3 2 1

For information about permission to reuse any material from this book please contact
The Permissions Company at www.permissionscompany.com or e-mail permdude@
gmail.com.

Publications by BOA Editions, Ltd.—a not-for-profit corporation under
section 501 (c) (3) of the United States Internal Revenue Code—are
made possible with funds from a variety of sources, including public
funds from the Literature Program of the National Endowment for
the Arts; the New York State Council on the Arts, a state agency;
and the County of Monroe, NY. Private funding sources include
the Lannan Foundation for support of the Lannan Translations
Selection Series; the Max and Marian Farash Charitable Founda-
tion; the Mary S. Mulligan Charitable Trust; the Rochester Area
Community Foundation; the Steeple-Jack Fund; the Ames-Amzalak Memorial Trust in
memory of Henry Ames, Semon Amzalak, and Dan Amzalak; and contributions from many
individuals nationwide. See Colophon on page 116 for special individual acknowledgments.

ART WORKS.
arts.gov

State of the Arts

NYSCA

Cover Design: Sandy Knight
Cover Art: *Copper Beech 62"*, copyright © by Benjamin Swett
Interior Design and Composition: Richard Foerster
BOA Logo: Mirko

Library of Congress Cataloging-in-Publication Data

Names: Dobyns, Stephen, 1941- author.
Title: The day's last light reddens the leaves of the copper beech : poems /
    by Stephen Dobyns.
Description: First edition. | Rochester, NY : BOA Editions Ltd., 2016.
Identifiers: LCCN 2016019091 (print) | LCCN 2016024012 (ebook) | ISBN
        9781942683162 | ISBN 9781942683179 (ebook)
Subjects: | BISAC: POETRY / American / General.
Classification: LCC PS3554.O2 A6 2016 (print) | LCC PS3554.O2 (ebook) | DDC
    811/.54—dc23
LC record available at https://lccn.loc.gov/2016019091

BOA Editions, Ltd.
250 North Goodman Street, Suite 306
Rochester, NY 14607
www.boaeditions.org
A. Poulin, Jr., Founder (1938–1996)

Shimer friends: Peter Cooley and Peter Havholm

Contents

Part Three

Part Four
Reversals

Part Five

PART ONE

Stories

All stories are sad when they reach their end.
The rain comes; the night falls; Malone dies alone.
With little bites, the pragmatic devours the idealistic.
A bit of ash, a grain of sand; dust blows down the avenues.
Only yesterday the world shook its pom-poms;
roads extended their promise under an azure sky:
here an oasis, there an oasis, fat dawdles in between.
Pulled down from their branches, the hours
were quickly tasted and tossed away. What's this,
clouds on the horizon, or do we need glasses?
Between the countries of Arriving and Leaving,
no frontier, no change in the weather till later.
The murmuring, unruly mob lumbering behind;
the walls each morning yellowed by setting sun.

Stars

The man took the wrong fork in the road.
It was out in the country. They saw
no signs. It was getting dark. They began
to blame each other. Should they keep

going straight or should they turn around?
They drove past farms without lights.
The man said, If we reach a crossroad,
we can just turn right. His wife said,

I think you should turn around. The man
was driving. They kept going straight.
There's got to be a road up here someplace,
he said. His wife didn't answer. By now

it was pitch black. In their lights, the trees,
pressing close to the road, looked like people
wanting to speak, but thinking better of it.
The farther they drove, the farther they got

from one another, until it seemed they sat
in two separate cars. Who's this person
next to me? This thought came to them both.
They weren't newlyweds. They had children.

He's trying to upset me, thought the woman.
She thinks she always knows best, thought
the man. They were on their way to dinner
at a friend's farmhouse in the country. Now

they'd be late. It would take longer to go back
than to go straight, said the man. The woman
knew he hated it when she remained silent
so she said nothing. The woods were so thick

one could walk for miles and never get out.
The stars looked huge, as if they had come down
closer in the dark. The woman wanted to say
she could see no familiar constellations,

but she said nothing. The man wanted to say,
Get out of the car! Just to make her speak!
Where had they come to? They had driven
out of one world into another. They began

to recall remarks each had made in the past.
Only now did they realize their meanings,
hear their half-hidden barbs. They recalled
missing objects: a favorite vase, a picture

of his mother. How foolish to think they had
only been misplaced. They recalled remarks
made by friends before the wedding, remarks
that now seemed like warnings. Ice crystals

formed between them, a cold so deep that only
an ice ax could shatter it. Who is this monster
I married? They both thought this. Soon they'd
think of lawyers and who would get the kids.

Then, through the trees, they saw a brightly lit house.
They had come the long way around. The man
parked behind the other cars and opened the door
for his wife. She took his arm as they walked

to the steps. They heard laughter. Their friends
were just sitting down at the table. On the porch
the man told his wife how good she looked,
while she fixed his tie. Both had a memory

of ugliness: a story told to them by somebody
they had never liked. As he opened the door,
she glanced upward and held him for a second.
How beautiful the stars look tonight, she said.

Wisdom

With the door shut the child sat in the closet
with his fingers pressed in his ears. Tell me
the truth, wasn't it wisdom? Hadn't he had

a sudden insight into the nature of the world?
One time my stepson in third grade refused
to take any more tests. His reason? If you take one,

they'll only give you another. Better call a halt
right now. He had caught on to the grownups'
stratagem to drag him into adulthood. What

was in it for him? he asked. Nothing nice.
Likewise the boy in the closet had become
temporarily resistant to the blandishments

of the world. Two hours later, his own body
turned against him and he crept downstairs
to dinner. But when his parents pointed out

the joys of growing up, he remained in doubt.
Who knew how the thought had come to him?
TV, a friend's chatter? Perhaps he had seen

a picture of a conveyor belt. Click, click—
so he'd go through life until he was dumped
on a trash heap. Or perhaps he had deduced

what he was leaving behind, the shift from
innocence to consequence, from protection
to fragility. Fortunately, stories like the boy

shutting himself up in the closet are scarce,
and his parents joked about it to their friends.
By now, I don't know, he's on his second or

third marriage, has a job that's made him rich,
but that time in the closet, five years old and
calculating what life was destined to deal out,

how different it must have seemed from what
he had ever imagined, so he made his decision
and crept into the closet, wasn't it wisdom?

Parable: Horse

He peered into the bar mirror over the bottles
of gin and whiskey. Yes, he thought, he really
did have a long face. Why hadn't he noticed it

before? But looking out of his moony eyes,
he rarely wondered how others saw him, since,
apart from mirrors, he rarely saw himself.

Sure he was tall, no surprise there. Walking
along city sidewalks, he felt that was why people
slid to a stop when they saw him. But perhaps

it was his face that upset them, its odd expanse,
tombstone teeth, satchel mouth, black rubber lips.
People gawked and, glancing back, he saw

they were gawking still. None of this was new.
Yet each occasion once more fueled his sense
of isolation, which had begun at birth and came

from being an only child. He had no memory
of his father. His mother ran off after a few weeks
and he'd been raised by strangers. Stubbornly,

he worked to be strong, get on with the business
of living, to focus his thoughts on the road ahead.
But then a cruel wisecrack or brutal snicker

would tumble him back to the beginning again,
the self-doubt and crushing solitude. Did it really
matter if he had a long face? But it wasn't just that,

it was his whole cluster of body parts. Alone they
might have been fine, even the boxy feet. Then,
when all joined into the oneness that was him,

it changed. Not only did people stare, they looked
offended; as if his very presence upset their pride
and sense of self-worth; as if they were saying, How

can it be good fortune for *us* to walk here, if you
walk here as well; as if to see him and smell him
lessened them as human beings. Soon they'd brood

about their failings: broken marriages, runaway kids.
Was this his only power, to make others feel lesser?
How many of these downcast do we see on the street

whose insides are marked by scars, who show off
their apparent good cheer and lack of concern only
to conceal their fears? And even if we saw them

what could we do? The bartender coughed to get
his attention, half-grinning, half-appalled.
Why shouldn't he stay? He had no one to visit,

no place to go; he had only these long afternoons
in anonymous bars with the televisions turned low.
Give me a Jack Daniels, he said, and put it in a bowl.

Mrs. Brewster's Second Grade Class Picture

That's me, standing in the third row
with a wiseacre grin, skinny and blond,
taller than the others. Of the rest, George
and Jane, Jacqueline and Tom, a class

of sixteen and I recall nearly all the names:
the boys in white shirts or plaid; the girls
in skirts and bobby socks. Mrs. Brewster
stands to the right, dark hair, a benign smile.

She, who I'd thought old, looks about forty:
Bailey School, East Lansing, Michigan.
By now roughly sixty years have passed,
while the lives that, in 1948, were scarcely

at the start of life have almost completed
their separate arcs, if they haven't done so
already. Strange to think that some are dead.
A few of these children had great success,

a few had moderate triumphs, others
were dismal failures. Some were granted
happiness each day they spent on earth;
some felt regret with every step. I know

nothing of how their lives turned out.
Look at Margaret sitting cross-legged
in the front row in a light-colored dress.
The black and white photograph can't

do justice to her fine red hair. A smile
still uncorrupted by appetite or cunning,
no telling how long it retained its luster.
But all must have pursued life with various

degrees of passion, arrived at decisions
they felt the only ones possible to make.
How many would now think otherwise,
that the indispensable trip to Phoenix

might as easily have been to New York,
that the choice of a career in law might
just as well have been a job in a bank?
What is needed after all? Which choices

are the ones really necessary? Could I
have been as happy as a doctor or even
a cop? No burning passion lies hidden
in these faces, all that came later, if it

came at all. But how bright and eager
they appear, how ready to get started.
One morning Mrs. Brewster gave us a treat,
showing her slides of Yellowstone Park.

In the dim light of drawn shades we stared
at a buffalo calf crossing a brook, a bald eagle
perched on a dead branch, Fire Hole River,
Mystic Falls, Old Faithful of course. How strange

these places looked compared to where we lived.
Were these the wonders we'd been promised?
At the water's edge a grizzly devours the carcass
of an elk; a black wolf creeps out of the pines.

Furniture

How devious is our perception of rapidity.
The facial movements of human beings
skitter about like the flight of swallows.

The facial movements of tables and chairs
are more discreet in their outward gestures.
Such is the case with all inanimate objects.

The foolish would say that stationary objects
remain stationary. This is false. They move
a little faster than raindrops sculpt a rock.

Why hurry? What is won by hasty action?
This is why you never see a chair quarreling
with another chair; rather, they contemplate

the virtues of passivity, which is the reason
chairs are so very kind, tables also. They see
human beings as only a blur as we rush and

rush and then arrive at our end. They see us
as we might see a speeding bullet. You ask
what persistent thought has brought them?

They arrive at certainty before, not after,
an event. They have solved the problem
of unexpected results from random causes.

They have discovered the square root of pi.
Most of all, their work has shown them the path
of inflexible humility. Humbly, they let us

knock them about, stack them in a corner,
sell them from an auction block. Yet always
they offer us the other cheek. Let us study

their calm to become stronger, hiding desire
as disinterest, guile as composure. But no,
they don't like us; they have never liked us.

Water-Ski

The gift of putting something down, he had yet to discover it—letting it slide from his grip. You'd think it would be easy; an opening of the fingers and the person, humiliation, failure would float away. Instead, he kept going over the details, the variations and possibilities; what would have happened if he had done this or that. And so the ill-fated event occurred not once but a thousand times. He recalled those occasions years before when he'd tried to water-ski. There was always a moment after he fell when he hesitated to release the rope and was dragged roughly over the surface of the water. It was like that now. Let go, let go, he shouted to himself, as the hard surface of what he called his life pummeled and raked his skin.

Leaf Blowers

That autumn morning he awoke to the crying
of lost souls that quickly changed to the roar
of leaf blowers up and down the block. Still,
the lost souls hung on, although only as idea,
as if the day's cloudy translucence had become
the gathered dead circling the earth. Nothing
he believed, of course, but the thought gave flesh
to the skeletal lack, who assumed their places
on imaginary chairs and couches: acquaintances,
old friends, relatives, as impatient as patients
in a doctor's waiting room, an internist late
from a martini lunch.
                                  Yet it was him, his attention
they seemed to crave. Did it matter they were false?
They were real as long as he imagined them.
And their seeming need for him, surely the opposite
was true, as if they formed the ropes and stakes
tying down the immense circus tent of his past,
till, as he aged, the world existed more as pretext
to bring to mind the ones who had disappeared.
This morning it was leaf blowers, in the afternoon
it might be something else, so as time went by
the palpability of what was not, came to outstrip
the formerly glittering quotidian, till all was seem,
seem, ensuring that his final departure would be
as slight as a skip or jump across a sidewalk's crack,
perhaps on a fall morning with sunlight streaking
the maples' fading abundance. Afternoon, evening,
even in the dead of night, waking to clutch his pillow
as he slipped across from one darkness to the next.

Parable: Heaven

At first it seemed as nice as the real Heaven—
a little eating, a little fucking, a little nap,
then a little eating again, the cycle repeating
over and over. But maybe Forever would be

too much, even a century would be a struggle,
even a year. In time the fun would begin to pale—
a little eating, a little fucking, a little nap. Sure,
the others were terribly nice, if not too quick

in the head at least. Lush fields, oaks in full leaf—
a veritable Garden of Eden. In the nursing home,
when she and Rosie had discussed the option
of Heaven, each swore if she were taken first,

she'd come back to tell the other what it was like.
But Heaven meant being a rabbit in Wisconsin.
Wouldn't she be ashamed to visit Rosie now?
Even if she hurried back to the nursing home,

she was sure to be caught and wind up in a stew.
Negative thoughts, too many negative thoughts:
It was her duty to focus on the bright side of life.
Who cared if she'd had affairs, lied to her friends,

took money from the till or keyed the car doors
of folks she disliked, wasn't this human nature?
After all, millions were clearly more sinful than she.
So it stood to reason she'd be forgiven. But when

a hawk snatched up a new friend, she understood
why this spot meant giving birth to a constant
supply of bunnies—a little eating, a little fucking,
a little nap. No wonder her friends were jittery

and their noses twitched; no wonder they were
speedy runners with foxes and coyotes lurking
in the underbrush. Eating, fucking, and napping,
wasn't it just self-medicating? So as she popped

out litter after litter, she began to ask: When
would it happen to her? When the fox's teeth
clamped vise-like on her neck or she heard
the owl's plunging rush of wings, would she

then find herself in the fleecy clouds of Heaven—
the hallelujahs, perpetual singing, the regular sex—
or had she mistaken her location from the start
and she'd come back as a spider, maybe a snake?

Good Days

Jack McCarthy, Stand-Up Poet, 1939–2013

It had been one of those good days with friends
and now we were sitting around the bonfire
telling stories—a circle of light within the dark.

The wind through the trees above us sounded
like faraway conversations, perhaps the talk
of friends around bonfires in the past. Some

were drinking, some not. Some leaned back
on their elbows, some sat cross-legged.
You know how it is: your face grows hot,

your back turns cold. As time passed, one
by one, men and women got to their feet and
walked into the night. Yes, that's how it was.

Part Two
Sixteen Sonnets for Isabel

Monochrome

The day I learned my wife was dying
it was September. Trees were green,
now they turned brown; flowers dimmed;
to recall their color seemed a mockery.

This was the first of the changes, then came
the slow shift to monochrome,
as all of nature commenced to bleed out
and take on the face of an overcast sky.

Unaccountably, people kept walking around.
They shopped; they partied. I called to them:
Hide in your basements! Try to stay warm!
Some laughed; some scratched their heads.

Then I knew the world wasn't broken;
my eyes were broken.

Song

The day I learned my wife was dying
is farther away than the fall of Rome
and as close as the next second.
It's dread promise fills every moment.

Birds mouth their songs; I hear no sound.
The air is heavy; they can hardly fly.
Everything is upside down. Sparrows
and robins line up on the wires. Then one

tumbles to the ground. Some days, I think,
I'm only a half step from surrender. In Rome,
songbirds' tongues were a delicacy. Eating them,
people mouthed their songs, hoping to sing,

as I do now. Grunts, rasps, croaks, gasps:
this isn't their song; it's my song.

Technology

The day I learned my wife was dying
she and I changed from one statistic
to another. Computers made the adjustment,
hummed a little, then settled down again.

The hum conveyed no misery or grief,
which was a big step for us all, because
formerly a clerk marking a sheet might
recall his own familiar absences and blot

his paper with a salty drop. How foolish
life was in the old days. Technology makes
it simpler; nasty events can be modified
by smart machinery and nothing need be

"hands on" anymore. With a single keystroke,
the worrisome page again becomes virginal.

Skyrocket

The day I learned my wife was dying
I tried to think it was a kind of hurrying-up,
since, of course, our first breath after birth
is the start of our dying. I told myself

death is part of life. I was full of lies.
I tried to put something between me
and the fact of her illness: maybe a wall,
maybe the obliteration of perception.

Nothing worked. As the world got dimmer,
her death grew brighter, nosier; it zigzagged
about the house like a frantic rocket. That's
how it seemed. I wanted a little quiet

for productive thought, but as time passed
I knew it was best to keep my mind blank.

Lizard

The day I learned my wife was dying
I thought, What about me? Then I grabbed
the virtual hammer I always keep with me
and whacked myself over the head.

I was like a pup tent in Manhattan.
I wasn't the subject of the sentence;
I wasn't even *in* the sentence. A beer
can bobbing in the ocean, that was me.

Her illness eased its lizard body into our home,
slid its vastness across chairs and left slime
on the walls till nothing was familiar anymore.
It's red tongue flicked and we ran. My wife didn't run.

She tried to teach us acceptance. But we, as foolish
as ever, wanted tools to fight it, not acceptance.

Swap Shop

The day I learned my wife was dying
the knowledge became a leash clipped
to my collar, a leash in the paw of her illness,
which rose tall above me; and if I thought

of a book, ball game, or chicken dinner,
the leash would be given a sharp yank
to show who was in charge, and whack me
with the fact of her dying. I wore the leash

all day; I wore it at work and when I slept;
I wore it in the shower. A single step
in the wrong direction put it in action
and I'd be flat on my back. You know those

dodgy trade-offs in swap shops? It was like that:
all my thoughts traded for the one I dreaded.

Alien Skin

The day I learned my wife was dying
I began to hear of her illness all over.
People in carwashes and barbershops had it,
friends, acquaintances, even enemies had it.

On TV it was the topic of panel discussions;
its name lurked at the foot of all conversations.
I felt confused; it was as if these others existed
to diminish my wife's individual pain, as if

her illness were less serious by being in a crowd.
But we knew hers was the worst. All the family
knew that. And what we knew was like a layer
of alien skin and we scratched at its scaly presence.

But it never bled, no matter how hard we scratched;
rather, to mock our good health, it turned rosy.

Pain

The day I learned my wife was dying
I thought of the interior pain of those
who loved her, starting with me.
But no x-ray machine would show it;

pills, operations, nothing could prove it.
The people who loved her would look
perfectly healthy. I'm not really, I'd say,
I'm really very sick. Ditto all the others.

Perhaps we could hold up signs describing
just where we hurt; or wrap ourselves
in bloody bandages, use crutches and canes
to explain the degree of our interior pain.

Friends might guess my mountain of loss,
but I'd buy ads on TV to tell strangers.

Niagara Falls

The day I learned my wife was dying
I thought of all the words we'd never speak.
Not just *I love you* or *let's go for a walk*,
but complaints and words from fights.

How much I'd give to have her to tell me
take out the garbage, pick up your books!
I'd be eager to see her angry again; I'd accept
any slight or defamation of character.

But like the world on old maps, up ahead
loomed a cataract. As at Niagara, folks
with telescopes might watch us float by
as we, in our barrel, bobbed toward it. How

feeble is language! Where were the words
to turn this to a story to make her laugh?

The Wide Variety

The day I learned my wife was dying
I wanted to think it was somebody's fault.
Big business, chemical toxins or perhaps
it was the fault of the man up the street.

If that were the case, I'd give him a smack.
But I had no one to blame; no one to punish.
So what could I do with my anger? Could I
hurl stones at the sky, polish my whimper?

It's depressing to have no one to blame,
to sit beside her with no solution, nothing
to fix. I needed villains, like demons in antique
paintings plaguing a saint. But these days

that wide variety is internalized: the vicious,
good and malignant, all find a place within us.

Skin

The day I learned my wife was dying
I touched the back of my hand gently
to her cheek. How warm it felt.
What will it be like when it's not?

To find out I took bags of green beans
from the freezer, stuck my finger
in ice cream to feel the cold, but
I couldn't get the temperature right.

But no, all that's a lie. How paralyzing
becomes bad news. I felt I knew exactly
what her skin would be like. I couldn't
stop thinking about it. And whatever

I guessed, it would be worse; and can I
guess the color? There will be no color.

Never

The day I learned my wife was dying
I went to read about volcanic eruptions,
earthquakes, fire, bloody war, and murder.
I wanted to discover the most awful, because

I knew her death would be worse than that;
and even crueler would be her absence, not
for a day or a year. It meant not coming back.
That was what I couldn't imagine. How many

days in Never? How many times would we
hear a car and think, That's her, or hear
the phone ring and feel suddenly happy,
only to grasp it was basically nobody,

and each burst of knowing would be one
little death, and they will happen all day.

Casserole

The day I learned my wife was dying
friends called to see if we needed anything
and if they could help out. Just what
do you have in mind? I wanted to ask.

Even if I got hard drugs, I'd eventually
wake up. And there it would be again:
the awful knowing. Compared to that
could I ask for a casserole? The richest

of the world's gifts wouldn't mean squat.
To know friends' feelings helped a little,
but afterward the pain was just as great.
What could they do to fill a vacancy?

At most we had a shared helplessness;
naïve victims of how the world works.

Inexplicably

The day I learned my wife was dying
I began to study alternative universes.
In my house, life might be fucked up,
but somewhere existed a place where

she wouldn't be tired or need morphine.
We wouldn't be figuring out how many
days she had left. Sure, we couldn't fly
to such a world, but just to know it existed

might help. I'd think of her reading a book
or pruning the roses. When the phone rang,
I'd say it was she and be right. How good
you look, people would say, and I would too.

Then we might kiss and visit those crannies
that, inexplicably, we had left untouched.

Prague

The day I learned my wife was dying
I told myself if anyone said, Well, she had
a good life, I'd punch him in the nose.
How much life represents a good life?

Maybe a hundred years, which would
give us nearly forty more to visit Oslo
and take the train to Vladivostok,
learn German to read Thomas Mann

in the original. Even more baseball games,
more days at the beach and the baking
of more walnut cakes for family birthdays.
How much time is enough time? How much

is needed for all those unspent kisses,
those slow walks along cobbled streets?

Gardens

The day I learned my wife was dying
I thought of how knowledge is finite
while imagination has no end. It's like
the earth versus the universe; and once

out there, why come home? But I've no choice;
the imagination abruptly sags, and plop,
I'm here again, and everything's worse.
This happens dozens of times each day.

I expect those who are mad are stuck
on imagination's side and can't get back.
I've come to envy them: to flee the Awful
for what the mind constructs: impossible

gardens with books and good things to eat.
And she'll be there, healthy and laughing.

Part Three

The Miracle of Birth

For Sylvia Lee

Hacking and coughing, slapping at scorch marks
on their otherwise white robes, the souls
of the dead stagger toward the Pearly Gates
as St. Peter tugs his beard to hide a guilty look.

Oh, how they loved them; how could they ever
exist without them? So do the souls clamor over
their absent anatomy. Only a cynic would claim
the souls of the dead ascend with the last gasp

of breath. Instead, like a faithful hound curled
in the grass by its master's tomb, the souls
try to hang on, sneaking into coffins, hitching
rides to crematoriums, anything to win a last

embrace from a dear one. But then the smell
begins: fetor of decay, miasma of putrefaction.
Press an ear to the bare earth of a fresh grave
and soon you'll hear a familiar choking sound.

A day later a nighttime jogger might spot a geyser
of marsh gas or will-o'-the-wisp, as the gagging
guardian of the recently defunct blasts off toward
the balmy air of heaven. Even faster is their escape

from crematoriums as eruptions of greasy smoke
racing skyward readily attest. But just as the folks
at refineries mix methyl mercaptan with odorless
propane to create the stink of rotten eggs, skunk

smell, robust farts, so the powers of heaven splash
a suitable stench on the moldering flesh. Otherwise

a soul might linger until only the chromium balls
and polyethylene sockets of phony hips remained.

Thus the nasty smell. Those kids practicing kisses
or couples fucking in the backseats of VW bugs
are amorous triflers compared to the ardor of the soul
for its partner. As they sullenly wait for reassignment,

they dangle their feet into the blue abyss at the brink
of heaven like boys on a wall bumping their sneakers
on the bricks below. Isn't it the soul's initial distaste
for its next host and its loyalty to the past that leads

to the mix-up of childhood and tumult of adolescence?
Such is the miracle of birth as the soul is first thrust
into a minuscule egg, then cast squawking into the world
as potential rich man, poor man, beggar man, thief.

Fly

What's that noise? a man asks his wife.
She walks to the window. The sound of feet,
thousands of boots marching in unison.

I can see nothing, the woman tells him.
The man joins her. Nothing, he repeats.
And the smell—think of the smell of one

unwashed body, one unwashed uniform,
and increase it a hundred thousand fold.
The man shuts the window, but still the smell

sticks to their skin, clings to every part
of their home. What is it? the man repeats.
Their voices are no more than a whisper.

They can hide. What's the point of hiding?
They can run. Why bother running?
They feel defeated by the world's terrors.

They can turn up their radio and dance.
They can play cards; they can drink gin.
They can fight one another or make love.

It will be there even still. A fly crawls
across the window. The man squashes it
with his thumb. Like them, like them.

The Inquisitor

Arriving home, he rubs his hands
to warm them up or work out the kinks,
I don't know which. Next he greets

the wife with a smack on the cheek
and gets one back in the give and take
of domestic bliss. After that he checks

the mirror to inspect his smile. Which
looks best, when he shows off his teeth
or not? He scrubs his hands with a stiff

brush, good soap. If hands could shine
this would be the time, but they're as pale
as parchment or a worm beneath a rock.

A nice roast for dinner, not too rare,
sliced beets, chopped cabbage, asparagus
spears, then a fat cigar before the fire.

He would never think of kicking his dog;
the cat is safe on his lap. As for plucking
the wings off flies, he's not that sort.

His children without exception get
the best Christmas and birthday gifts,
toy cop cars with flashing lights, dolls

that shed real tears. Quick to loan
a friend a hammer or cordless drill.
Quick to join the blood drive or pledge

a sawbuck to the policemen's ball.
On Sundays it's yard work, cutting the grass,
chopping a hedge. He's good with tools

and might sharpen a neighbor's ax.
At night he and the wife relax in front
of the TV with popcorn and beer—

tragedies and butchery, the usual fare.
What's this nonsense? The screen is dark.
All the stories float in the air in between.

The Poet's Disregard

Once more Old Anonymous picks up his pen.
What shall he write about this time?
The eternal verities have turned out
less than eternal. Once again endless love

has ended. He ponders composing an ode
to his long time sidekick Death, but as his
own departure draws near their friendship
has grown problematic. The pen of the poet

hangs in mid-air like an arrested rocket.
The world in a grain of sand, the worm
in the heart of the rose—the old subjects
in slinky gowns execute their turns along

the runway of his imagination. At times,
Anonymous thinks, it's necessary to wait,
and then wait some more. Clocks gobble
minutes like salted nuts as today's struggle

between the brutal and pragmatic flails away
a stone's throw from the poet's disregard,
by the glare of the burning library,
beneath the shadow of the deserted school.

Parable: Gratitude

At times virtue is a torture, kindness a crime.
Think of the pig whose right rear leg was made
of solid wood; straps on his belly kept it in place.

But isn't this the pig that saved the farmer's kids
from the river? Hadn't he fixed the timing belt
on the farmer's Ford? The farmer patted the pig

on the head, gave him a smooch on the snout.
But to a friend he said: A pig like that you don't
eat him all at once. Soon a second leg was gone.

The pig shingled the roof, painted the house,
dug a new well. The farmer gave him cookies
and let him sleep in a featherbed, but the farmer

began grinding his teeth. He had headaches
and peculiar fits of temper. He asked himself:
Have I gone nuts seeing all the pig has done?

The pig milked the cows, made cider, pickled
cucumbers and beets, canned the kumquats.
Soon the farmer had trouble sleeping at night;

he quarreled with his wife, yelled at the kids.
What's the farmer's problem anyway? Such
is the burden of emotional debt. Each step

he took felt like a spike through his foot. His life
became a minus sign, a spot well below zero.
When the friend came back, the pig's front legs

had been turned to hams and he was strapped
to a kid's skateboard. I'm saving the best for last,
the farmer joked. The pig sang to the hens so they

laid more eggs. He taught the kids to yodel Bach.
The storm cloud above the farmer's head grew
to the size of Texas. He felt worse than sludge

at the bottom of a well. Soon the pig was gone.
Good to the last drop, the farmer told his friend.
Right away, his house began to fall apart;

the barn roof collapsed; a fox ate the chickens.
The farmer welcomed each crisis with a smile.
He slept like a baby. His sex-life grew robust.

On a tombstone by the barn were the words:
This was one smart pig! Freed from the curse
of obligation, the farmer polished his vulgarity;

he drank straight from a bottle and shot craps
with his friends. His spouse played sex games
with the gas man; the kids gulped down mind-

confounding drugs. Each felt reborn. Is this
what we call normal? They splashed about
in the great, warm bath of milk called happiness.

They lounged about in the jubilation of disregard.
Virtue became a nasty word like *dog-shit* or *fart*.
The kids tossed rocks at every truck that passed.

Sincerity

Today I'll write a poem about myself—
not like the other poems I've written
about myself. No, this one will be more
truthful, or at least more sincere. It's my
sincere self that's writing today, the self

that longs for intimacy, or some intimacy,
at least. My sincere self says: I work hard;
I try the best I can; I'm often a good person.
But today the self I'm writing about is also
more likable than the self I wrote about

yesterday, not silly-likable or I'll-give-you-
money likable, but trustworthy likable;
that is, more trustworthy than not, trust-
worthy enough to be trusted. I want to be
completely honest about this. I want you

to see me ripping off my clothes and rising
before you shy and vulnerable, prepared
to tell my deepest secrets, or deep enough
for you to think they're hugely deep, which
they will be, most of them, more than half.

I want you to see me on the brink of tears,
my whole body on the brink of tears,
elbows on the brink of tears, my feet,
my thumbs, my earlobes, my hair follicles,
even my genitals on the brink of tears,

each testicle on the brink of tears, big
ball, little ball, and each totally sincere.
I don't want any confusion about this.

I know at times I've stretched the truth.
For example, my dysfunctional childhood,

that spanking I once told you about had,
indeed, no sexual component. That time
I fell down stairs? I shouldn't have said
I was pushed. And my sexual conquests?
My last girlfriend said I should have been

a monk; she said it would have saved me
years of embarrassment. In fact, she was
more a girl-acquaintance, than a girlfriend,
someone I sat next to on a crosstown bus.
So she's not the one who matters here. I'm

the one who matters. I want you to see me
with my arms outstretched to reveal truth
stripped of hyperbole and sexual overkill,
as sincerity throbs like an exposed artery. Soon
I'll recount my trials and beating the odds,

but as we wait for the big subjects to roll out
grant me a microscopic sweetness squeezed
from the golden cornucopia orbiting above us.
May I lay my head on your shoulder? Then,
of course, you too will have the chance to share.

Hero

This is what happened: a man needed a job.
He hadn't worked for a month so he took
the civil service exam and got a job
at the Detroit zoo, way down the totem pole,

right at the bottom. He wore blue overalls
and a blue cap. He looked like a cop without
the badges and Glock. His job was to feed
the zebras, feed the giraffe, feed the bears.

The bears' cage resembled a stone cave
without a roof. But it had a ledge about
six feet off the ground. His boss said:
Sometimes a bear likes to get on the ledge

and jump on whoever is giving him food.
It hasn't happened much, but it's happened.
So keep alert. The next morning the man fed
the zebras, he fed the antelopes and giraffes.

When he got to the bears' cage, he paused.
No bears in sight. The man entered the cage
and took a step toward the feeding trough,
then he took one more. Only ten steps to go.

Still no bear. It must be waiting nearby. Soon
he heard a noise—maybe a bear, maybe a bus
on Woodward Avenue. What was his chance
of being eaten? The man's legs were as heavy

as tombstones. He thought of home; he thought
of his wife and six kids. He wasn't very big.
He knew what bears could do to a little guy
like him. They would gobble even his buttons.

Time passed. People looked into the cage, but
saw no bears, only a keeper standing as stiff
as a flagpole. Could he run to the trough, dump
in the food and run back? Of course he could.

But he was a thinker, that was the problem.
He had a gift for spotting nasty scenarios.
As in a movie, he could see the bear hurl itself
from the ledge. That would be just the start.

Way in the back a small black bear woke up.
He was hungry. It was way past feeding time.
The bear took a peek over the ledge. No food.
He growled. Still no food. He reared up on his

hind legs and roared like an Alaskan grizzly.
Hadn't the man known this would happen?
He dropped the pail and ran to the bus stop.
He even forgot to change out of his uniform.

Close call, he told himself. It wasn't exactly
courage, but it was good enough. After all,
he was alive. He began to tell people the story
of how he had escaped from a bear. With each

retelling the bear grew bigger, then it was
two bears. He showed a scar on his arm from
an old bike accident as a kid. This was where
the bear clawed him. The man had no doubt

he was telling the truth. In time, he developed
an aura of quiet strength; he spoke modestly
about being a hero. His kids looked up to him.
His wife kissed his cheek. Does it matter what

really took place? These reversals of bad luck
that fate confers on the seemingly unworthy,
they offer us hope and help us through
the dark places; they let us greet the night.

Statistical Norm

He was amazed by the curve of his life. What he had thought unique had made its arc like any other, as if life had conspired to deny him his genius. His differences, finally, were very slight—like a man preferring chocolate to vanilla. His youth, education, career, his friendships, the ties to his family, even illnesses—there was nothing exceptional. And as he neared his end, he saw that here too he would yield to a statistical norm more offensive than death itself: a grave in a row of graves, his ashes mixed with the ashes of others. In his youth, he had written poetry, worn black, spoken of the avant-garde—no trace of that person remained. But he pictured him still walking the streets of some city, pursuing his passions. These days, as he puttered about, he liked to imagine the young man's fabled successes: the women who sat at his feet, the men who stepped aside as he entered a room. Then all would look toward him as he prepared to speak. A hush would fall. And that was the problem, wasn't it? For when he tried to call up his deepest thoughts, the rich complexity of his convictions, what could he have said?

Turd

The only time I hit a boy in the face surprised us both.
He was flailing; I was flailing. We weren't joking around.
This was in fifth grade sixty years ago and I haven't
seen him since. Who knows how his life worked out?
In those days being a writer was on the back burner,
and being a jet pilot seemed a better choice, perhaps
a private detective. Where I was and where I wanted
to be were two islands separated by miles of water.
I'd stand on my imagined shore and scratch my head;
lots of time passed like that. So I hit him, poked a knuckle
in his eye, and everything stopped. I've forgotten what
the fight was about. This happened in the boy's dorm
at Clear Lake Camp—rows of bunk beds for fifty kids
and all cheered us on. When I hit his eye, he yelped:
He hit me! He wasn't giving credit where credit was due.
It was an accident. He was appalled; I was appalled.
The boy began to weep and I began to weep as well.
He was nobody I knew; he went to a different school.
Boys from my school kept pounding me on the back;
boys from his school led him away. And that was that.
But this is just the start of the story. We were there
for a fall weekend, and before lunch the men in charge
gathered us together for an announcement. We knew
something big was coming; we saw it in their faces:
a mixture of moral horror and righteous indignation.
This was in 1951 and six of the men were vets. D-Day,
Okinawa, they'd seen it all. At first I thought the reason
for the meeting was my fight that morning. I was sure
the kid had told and I'd be called out. Instead we heard
that some unknown boy had left an oversized turd
in the middle of the shower room: twelve showers,
a floor of pink tile and the turd, six inches long,
squatting like a toad in the middle. I know this
because the teachers paraded us through single-file.

The word "turd" was never used, that's my addition.
Shit, crap, dump, poop, caca, ass goblin, black banana,
hell's candy, creamy butt nugget, keester cake, lawn
sausage—none of this was said. The phrase of choice
was that an unknown boy had crept into the shower
and "moved his bowels," as he might move an elephant.
He had left his BM on the pink tiles. We were children.
What we knew about the war was comic book stuff,
so the product of one bad boy's moved bowel viewed
through the filter of adult displeasure seemed equal
to Judas' betrayal and the bombing of Pearl Harbor.
The lecture was long and operatic. Nobody owned up.
At last Mr. Sullivan placed a small desk and chair near
the monstrosity, as outside the shower room fifty boys
formed an anxious line. Each was to enter and sit down,
as Mr. Sullivan, standing above him, shouted: Does that
belong to you? I won't get mad if you tell me the truth!
Despite my innocence, I was sure my guilt would show.
I was sure I'd giggle. I was sure I'd weep. I was sure
I'd confess to punching a kid in the eye. But why stop
with one turd, the mere tip of ten years of bad behavior?
I'd spill out past sins like a fire hose spills out water.
I'd tell him I stole dollar bills from my mother's purse;
I'd tell him I searched my father's coat pockets for coins;
I was full of dirty thoughts; I'd begun to masturbate;
I'd killed a robin with a BB gun and buried the body
in my little brother's sandbox; I'd tried on my mother's
bra to see how it looked; I hid Hershey bars in my room;
I didn't believe in God, not one bit; I stole comic books
from supermarkets; I didn't return books to the library;
I once broke a girl's leg on the teeter-totter and ran away;
I'd spent two hours looking up "whore" in the frigging
dictionary not knowing it started with W. I was a bad boy.
I was born a bad boy. I'd die a bad boy. I was marooned
on the island of childhood like a degenerate sailor.
My only chance was to plead guilty and beg for mercy.
Mr. Sullivan asked his question. I couldn't look at him.

I shook my head. Then came a pause as long as January.
Next! he called, and a million birds began to whistle glory.
Nobody confessed. Buses took us back to East Lansing.
For all I know, the turd's still there. And shouldn't it be?
Shouldn't there be a little turd shrine to bullied children
and dumb ideas, to preadolescent confusion, to always
being uncertain and mostly being scared, to all those
kids who triple-lock the bathroom door and then check
the window, afraid of doing something right, of doing
something wrong, of getting caught, of getting away,
afraid of wearing the wrong-colored socks, afraid their
flies are unzipped, afraid they'll fart in class, a fart
like the tuba of John Philip Sousa, afraid of pee stains,
of reeking arm pits, of sudden projectile vomiting—
that's the sort of shrine they need and if that antique
turd is gone, I'd be happy to donate one of my own.

Parable: Friendship

Some tragedies are big; some very small.
Here's a parrot whose two feet were caught
in an elevator door. Doesn't this happen often?

He was humming a tune or thinking about lunch,
when his feet were snipped from his legs.
He was a flightless New Zealand Owl Parrot

named Buzzy, who was passed down over
sixty years to Ralphie, his present owner.
So how did he get by without feet? Buzzy

learned to grip his perch with his little red
parrot prick, allowing him to stay up late
with Ralphie over a beer and good baseball chat

before Ralphie left for work at midnight. But
his wife hated Buzzy and his little red prick,
and she didn't like Ralphie much either. You know

how these troubles begin. The wife took up
with a ne'er-do-well for sexual relief, and after
midnight the fellow snuck through the back door

so he and the wife could smooch on the couch
at least at the start. Then in the morning Buzzy
would give Ralphie the latest report: how

the lover and wife made the couch pulsate
like an earthquake as they probed the depths
of passion. But here's the sad part of the story.

One morning Ralphie found his friend with his head
tucked under his wing. What's up? said Ralphie.
Buzzy didn't speak. Tell me, said Ralphie. Nope,

croaked Buzzy. This went on till Ralphie swore
he'd lock his friend in a closet. Okay, said Buzzy,
first they kissed. Go on, said Ralphie. Next he

squeezed her breasts. It's not true! cried Ralphie.
It was a long story, better imagined than told.
At last the parrot squawked, Then he tore off

her lacy, pink thong. Keep going! cried Ralphie.
I can't, moaned Buzzy. Why not? said Ralphie.
Because, said the parrot, I fell off my perch.

Here the joke always stops. But who ever thinks
of the parrot's feelings? His job with Ralphie
was his first work in sixty years and he'd failed.

I did my best! cried Buzzy. But Ralphie no longer
bothered about Buzzy and his little red prick,
and he grabbed his hat and ran from the house.

Could Buzzy comfort his friend? Not a chance.
Consider how life can take a complete flip
in two seconds. First we've got the heavens,

then comes the abyss. Even if Ralphie forgave
the parrot, they'd share no more beer and
good baseball chat. He'd always see the hurt

in Ralphie's eye. The warmth would depart
from his heart. The parrot would be ignored.
Could he crawl to the street and be crushed

by a bus? Quite unlikely. Say he leapt to the floor,
what could he do? With just a little red prick
to navigate, he'd flop about like a trout out of water.

If this were the President, books would be written
on the subject. But since it's only a parrot why
should it matter? Days passed as Buzzy gazed

at the ceiling in confused thought: a brain full
of zeros, a heart full of holes. In a nicer world
Buzzy might get a tear or kindly pat on the back,

but now he's just a sob behind a closed door.
Let's face it. Who's blameless, who's blessed,
who's punished, who's cursed—it's a tossup.

The Dark Uncertainty

Often he tried to imagine the intimacy enjoyed by others, friendships of telepathic closeness, families bound lovingly like families in old movies—the parents caring, the children happy. And those groups of people picnicking in parks as he walked by on a path beneath the trees, or groups laughing together in restaurants—he pictured friends growing up together, being the support of one another through full lives, and then their funerals with long lines of automobiles traveling slowly with their lights on. He never thought these people might experience anxiety or doubt, that dark uncertainty could fill them with dread, that ambition or envy might lead them to compromise whatever ideals they had at the start. In fact, he never thought they might be like he was. Yet if he had, if he'd seen in others his own image, wouldn't his isolation have been decreased? If fear hadn't blurred his vision of the world, wouldn't he have found that he too had a place within it?

No Simple Thing

Not having as yet learned how to live—
indecision skittering like a dust devil
across appetite's parking lot—the time
has come to learn how to die. First

I'll put away my clothes, return my books
to their shelves; then I'll raise the blinds,
to see what's happening on the street
and which birds are forming their flocks,

since I think it will be fall with the trees
nearly bare, except for clusters of leaves
clinging to the oaks. Does it matter that
I've never learned to sleep on my back?

Soon I'll have plenty of time to practice.
Like people standing in line waiting for a train,
I'll check my watch against a clock on the wall,
touch the ticket tucked in my breast pocket.

Don't accuse me of morbidity. Actuarial tables
have quickened their work against me. Oh,
it's no simple thing to practice for death
and I've yet to reach the subject of goodbyes.

Will I have time to speak to the people I love,
to press a hand or stroke a cheek? Then each
might need to make some remark, maybe even
an ironic gesture, nothing too somber as could

complicate a rational occasion. Better, I think,
to slip out across the driveway to where a car
is waiting, its motor making the softest hum.
As often occurs the cat will escort me part way

and I'll bend to scratch his ears, as he stretches
to let me scratch his neck as well. I don't know
what birds will be left, I don't know if it will be
sunny or dark. Pausing, I'll pat my pockets to see

if I've got my keys, and then smile at my mistake.
No time now for whatever remains undone, no
time for regrets or good thoughts, no time perhaps—
and this is hard to imagine—even to shut my eyes.

Yes, this practicing for death is no simple thing—
look at how I open my hand and once or twice
flick my wrist so a bit of fluff or loose thread
stuck to my fingers can at last float away.

PART FOUR
Reversals

Narrative

A chunk of metal cubed and spat out
by a car-crushing bailing press, a Ford,
twenty years old, seemingly red, last
driven by a teenaged girl who'd failed
to check the oil, a gift from a doting

grandmother with a terror of squashing
squirrels recklessly crossing the road,
who drove the car only to church, after
buying the Ford at Ziggy's, a used car lot,
when repossessed from a single mom

who had missed her payments till Ziggy
got cross, a woman working at Wal-Mart
whose former significant other left when
he decided the Marines were his best option
after all, but had picked up the car cheap

from a couple who liked energetic sex
in the backseat and were forced to sell
when the baby came, the spot of conception
marked by a stubborn stain on the fabric
the shape of Texas, and the upshot being

a daughter about to complete high school;
a couple that had first bought the Ford
from a soap salesman eager for something
faster and jazzier; all but the salesman
still engaged with the world, at times

walking past one another on the street,
or entering a diner, buying a few roses,
or riding a bus, a group not quite
a family, but who shared a memory
of faulty brakes, stuck glove box,

interior lights that rarely worked,
seven people, including Ziggy,
strangers intimately linked, except
for the soap salesman, the first owner,
an erratic driver, dead now ten years.

Determination

Cabbage—the first word put down
with his new pen, a trophy pen,
like a trophy wife, not cheap,
absurd to use a ballpoint pen

for a task like this, a challenge,
for which he'd also bought a new,
but antique, rolltop desk recently
restored, with matching chair,

also not cheap, and for which
he'd renovated the attic room with
pine-paneled walls, bookshelves,
and a good light for his new office

or weekend office, a place planned
for many years, even before college,
back in high school in fact, a resolve
rare in his life, but about which

he'd dreamed in free moments
at work, and which kept him
sane during those tedious years
of doing the taxes for strangers,

but now at last begun, excitingly
begun, as he leaned forward with
pen raised to put down on paper
the first word of his first novel.

Jump

Then he trips and falls splat on the walk,
tangling his feet, jumping too quickly
from crack to crack, leaps that felt like
flying as he pushed off with red Keds,

sneakers got that morning with money
from collecting empties, selling seeds,
candy door to door, shoveling sidewalks
in winter, raking leaves and of course

help from those above, being how he
regards his mom and dad, those above,
sounding at once cordial, but distant,
which was how he liked it, a decent

separation from the ones who held
the other end of the leash, those above,
galloping down the block, knowing
the names of dogs in every house,

a few nice, a few not; feeling his body's
Superboy power when he had earlier
slammed open the front door, sprinted
across the porch and leapt with arms

outstretched; a fighter jet, nearly flying,
but only jumping, a boy leaping, having
not yet grasped the line that separates
what might happen from what might not.

What Happened?

Taking first a morsel of squash,
then a bit of bread—an elegant
gray rat with glossy pelt, steps
lightly across the compost heap,

his best loved spot, unaware
of the source of such largesse,
not having linked these gifts
to the mother who wears a path

from house to dump, or from
the disgusted to the grateful
as inside the house her toddler
flicks another splop of beets

onto the floor with carrots soon
to follow; what fills the child
with indignation is for the rat
attained ambition, a trickle down

bounty, or so the rich might
have us think as they dole out
peanuts to the poor, making
the mom a middle-class flunky

who believes she's doing goodly
work. Is this the case? Not quite.
Instead she asks what happened,
as she recalls photos from the past:

her son's birth, her wedding, college,
winding her way back to fourth grade,
to one of those frigid winter days
when half the kids are dreaming

and she maps out a future of slashing
through a tangle of Amazon jungle,
a deadly snake in one hand, eager
to capture a jaguar with the other.

Philosophy

Nihilism, but not in a negative
sense—such was his thought,
what else to call it? Like snow
inside a novelty snow globe,

vague possibility descended
from probability, descended
from likelihood and certainty.
Now not even air. Those great

words discussed in college—
truth, beauty, justice, which
had come to embarrass him,
like teasing bare-breasted

girls in postcards sent from
Polynesian islands that each
year he had found less likely;
absolutes faded like old shirts,

as still he tried to create from
stray thoughts as if out of wood-
chips and mud, the old certainties
he once loved, the believable lie.

Melodrama

A gunshot: the trigger so light
he'd hardly known he pulled it;
another man's pistol grabbed from
an antique table with clawed feet
that he had bought last week—

before the fight and her departure—
bought driving to Memphis, the late
honeymoon they had been planning,
not realizing the antique salesman
was such a rascal, the same rascal

who'd shown up at their wedding
in Knoxville, oh, two months back,
a wedding in an art gallery with
watercolors by his cousin, delicate,
gray landscapes of the Smokies,

the cousin who'd brought the friend
nobody knew, an antique dealer
who flirted with his wife, his bride,
a girl he had loved since high school,
since tenth-grade history, the teacher—

whose name he couldn't remember—
who he'd once helped change a tire
on her van when she broke down
high up on the parkway and where
the boy had stared across the valley,

as if at a string of tomorrows, their
abundant on-goingness to the haze-
shaded horizon, an April morning,
the valley with its meandering river,
white barns, cows like black pinpricks.

Exercise

Luckily, he hadn't broken his neck,
had fallen instead into tall grass
when he'd slipped from the saddle
after letting go the reins, an accident,
but even so his first time on a horse,

a ten-year-old gelding, chestnut
with one white stocking, guaranteed
to be slow and responsible along
the trails through the pine woods;
a stable they saw each day, driving

into the city where he still worked,
having sworn the previous evening
to change his life, but nothing too
drastic, only some mild exercise
to please his wife, who never quite

bullied him, who surely loved him,
and who, he knew, deserved better;
a small gesture taking less than half
an hour, because what was the word
she had shouted at him? Sedentary.

Failure

I'm sorry, I'm expecting someone else,
speaking as he stood in front of her table,
but not raising her head, as he stuttered,
May I, May I . . . sweat beading his brow,

having just nearly tripped over the curb,
as he stepped forward, intent on asking,
May I buy you lunch? . . . gasping for breath
from sprinting across four lanes packed

with cabs, which he had side-stepped
and leapt across, to frustrate their wish
to squash him flat, as he again repeated,
Would you join me tonight for dinner?—

and this after he'd been compelled to wait
for the turtle advance of an uptown bus,
the exhaust stranding him in an aggravated,
black cloud of expectation, as he practiced

the phrase, *I'd like to get to know you better,*
deciding this was best after he had first seen
her figure, a green blouse off one shoulder,
the very raison d'état of his departure from

the further curb with his eyes focused upon
her outside table, convinced his wisest course
was to break loose of all timidity and shout,
I want to screw you till the cows come home,

sweet cakes; since hadn't he been helpless
once he had seen her lovely and expectant—
robins twittering, tulips blooming—and his
ardent self all set to break out? He knew it.

Constantine XI

—May 29, 1453

And he was never seen on this earth again,
having rushed forward with sword raised
toward the crowd of Turks boiling through
the breach in the wall, after first casting off

his crown and purple robes, so to be taken
for a common soldier and thrown down
in a common grave, buried with the others
to keep the enemy from parading his head

proudly through the cities of their empire,
this being his only choice—*The city has
fallen and I remain alive.*—last of the last,
God's representative on earth, ruling

a fragment of a city, still the seat of Rome
after eleven centuries, his army just a sliver
the size of the enemy's hundred thousand,
some of his soldiers being priests, slaves,

shopkeepers, even women, still protecting
a scrapheap, once the richest, largest, and
most beautiful, to be sacked for three days,
universities destroyed, libraries destroyed,

palaces and churches, schools and gardens,
citizens hunted down and slaughtered.
What alternative but to rush forward?
Remember him when your time comes.

Literature

Just midnight. Footsteps stop
by the outside door. Inside
he keeps alert, feels the rapid
beating of his heart, listening

to feet scraping up the walk,
having heard a car door slam.
Who had he been expecting?
Nobody. He'd been reading

a novel by the fireplace, one
with scenes so violent they'd
stick in his head all week—
disembowelment, decapitation—

a book lent him by a neighbor
he'd never liked, who revved
his Harley Sunday mornings,
tossed around the trash cans;

a man with whom he'd fought only
this morning when his dog tore up
the black-eyed Susans, swearing
to murder the dog, which, for sure,

he'd never do, he only wanted
to scare the man, make him sweat,
but who that afternoon lent him
the book he couldn't put down

that seized him like a rope squeezing
his throat. To make up, the man said,
to clean the slate; a man unknown
to tell the truth, who'd formed a plan

as fearful as murder, a stranger
at his door late at night, a sudden
shriek, and a book to soften him up.
You'll love it, the neighbor said.

Jism

And shot his wad all over the wall,
but wasn't that bound to happen
in the pitch black room when he'd
missed the correct orifice and fell

back, and she whooshing beneath him
like an engine building steam; this being
the trouble with arousal, the paradox
of rushing ahead of himself, the hasty

projection and hapless failure, because
it wasn't the first time; and it took place
despite the pricey ointments, vitamins,
New Age meditation, stabs at distraction,

like imagining pushing a red Cadillac up
an icy parking ramp while the inevitable
debacle hung in the air like the dirigible
Hindenburg over Lakehurst, New Jersey,

before its own tumescence discharged
in flames; and so he quickly polished up
the old excuses: e.g., a superabundance
of passion, for didn't she bring to mind

Anita Ekberg frolicking in Trevi Fountain,
a splashing that did the reverse of putting
a damper on his ardor, or he might boast
he'd blasted a warning shot across her bows,

or he frets about making a racket, getting
decrepit, feeling carsick, smelly armpits,
a list falling from likely to silly, as his fearless
Don Juan is morphed into a figure of fun?

Valencia

For Stuart Phillips

Droplets of water hang from the rusted ceiling
inside the butcher's truck as clouds of steam
rise from six slick bodies, like prayers ascending
to an empty heaven; six bulls suspended upside

down from hooks, and stripped of their hides,
pink and wet, their black hooves jutting straight
out, like a lost argument's second thoughts,
heads sawn off, severed necks nearly touching

the mix of water and blood, the floor's lake:
accept this afterlife, the dead flesh still alight
from living exertion, vapor surrounded and
slashed open from where the pretty killers

had thrust their sharp points during a fifteen-
minute rush between certain accomplishment
and certain defeat; the work begun by a blare
of trumpets as the double doors banged open

and each creature took its turn—shiny, dark,
and self-assured—to charge a few steps into
the ring, then pause to acknowledge the crowd's
shout, their great heads erect, the needle-tips

of their horns pivoting left and right—how strange
we must have looked to them—their front legs
all but dancing over freshly swept sand, and eager,
surely eager, like someone at the start of life.

Thanks

For Rick Mann

Your friend grabbing your wrist, as he hung
from the rusty metal ladder, calling out, Do
you need help?—the ladder fixed by bolts

to the concrete abutment sticking into
the river above the falls, your fingernails
dragging bit by bit over the rough stone

with your legs at the lip of plunging water,
and you being powerless to pull them back,
the current being too strong, grasping that

you'd soon be swept into the white cauldron
below—the result of not seeing the current
was pulling you into the center of the river.

as you'd half-swum, half-floated, supposing
a few strokes would take you to shore. So
what did you think might happen out of all

the decreasing possibilities? Why, nothing
at all, as you stared up at blue sky and trees
coming into full leaf, because why think

in such glorious weather? So you didn't notice
you were gathering speed as you floated under
the small bridge; so you hadn't considered

anything but pleasure when you first waded
into the water, leaving your sandals on the bank,
the current no more than a gentle tug, a dip

before dinner, as you thought of the evening
ahead—your wife, a movie, a book—but not
of the river where many swam, but not past

the bridge; stepping into the river, secure
in your belief in ongoing tomorrows, which
was stupid, stupid, because soon you'd be

an instant from being swept over the falls.
Then would you still think you could determine
the end of an action at the start of an action

as you had done when drifting downstream,
because, really, what is the meaning of safety?
A dream, an ambition? Why, nothing at all.

PART FIVE

Persephone, Etc.

The man with silver hooks instead of hands
picks apart a pomegranate on a park bench
as the sun malingers about the sky. It is hot
in the plaza and royal palms bring no relief.

Wicked monkeys wank among the fronds.
See him as an ex-sailor whose risky ventures
gobbled up his tender digits. It's market day
and treasure seekers haggle over odds and ends.

Wasn't it near this spot that the son of Kronos
pursued his inamorata, holding out a handful
of shining seeds? The ex-sailor asks, Why not?
These are time's entropic diminishments.

As each person's golden age is turned to tin,
he sets another crimson morsel on his tongue.

Crazy Times

For Charles Baxter

Twelve murderers are eating their dinners,
veal cutlets and walnuts, pickled pigs' feet.
Somebody sticks his head through the door.
The inevitable question is asked.
Not me, says Biter; nor me, says Shooter.
We didn't do it, say Choker and Stabber.
Nor me, nor me, say all the others.
The door closes with a bang.
The bad chaps return to their meal,
shoveling in the food with both hands,
slurping their jaws as they chew,
swallowing with great gulps, then belching,
picking their teeth with the tips of their daggers.
Afterward they stagger to the door and lurch down
the street. Back to work! they happily shout.

And you, shopping or walking or simply standing still,
you'd better pick up your feet and hightail it home,
lock those deadbolt locks and crawl under the covers.
Your brothers and sisters are coming to get you,
the ones you had forgotten about,
the ones you should have thought about earlier.
Ring ding goes the doorbell. Welcome to crazy times.

[revision]

Parable: Fan/Paranoia

He knew from the start it wasn't a mistake,
that he'd been the only person singled out.
Running from the dark bar to the sunlit street,
he asked why he hadn't been more alert.

The sidewalk was packed, and people darted
from his path, their faces distorted by disgust.
He thought fifty people had been in the bar—
a lunchtime crowd. But forty-nine were ciphers,

out-of-work actors hired for the job, and who
loved their roles given their sobs and shrieks,
the beating of fists on the floor. Yesterday
it was a near escape from a bus; before that

a brick was dropped from a roof. And those
out of work actors, they showed their hatred
by their refusal to look at him, their refusal
to give any sign of the devastation to come.

What had caused their loathing? Maybe he'd
insulted someone, or hurt someone. He tried
to recall likely enemies: ex-girlfriends, former
employers. Stubbornly, he searched his past,

going back to when he first learned to walk.
The beds he had wet, the pants he had shat.
Once begun he couldn't stop as he recalled
the dildo hung from a girl's dress with a pin.

No wonder he never got dates and lost friends,
no wonder someone loathed him. Had he ever
been lucky or done anything right? For years
he had lurched from one blunder to the next.

Was change an option? Could he help being a jerk?
All he knew for certain was someone somewhere
had dedicated his life to getting even, someone
sneaking along behind him, or on the next block.

The people hurrying toward him looked fretful,
the ones running away looked faint. But weren't
there odd rewards? Didn't his caution sharpen
the world around him so that every blossom

grew brighter, and even those who took flight
at his approach displayed a clumsy splendor,
as revulsion broke open the cage of anonymity
and inhibition? He saw the fear in their faces

and found it dreadful, but it also set his heart
beating with unfamiliar pleasure. See the man
advancing in the yellow hardhat? See the glare
in his little pink eyes? Surely his belief that here

was one of his enemy's minions also gave delight.
So it didn't matter when the man shouted out
in a voice rising above the street: You look like
shit! In another life, they might have been friends.

Winter Wind

Whitecaps on the river—so fierce
is the day's wind: a crowd of people
waving hats in the air. They must be
waving goodbye. Not yet, he thinks,
best not to look. Chickadees flutter
among the branches of the juniper,
playing it safe. Who knows where
they might end up? Feathered confetti.
All night he dreamt of cars in collision;
someone's done for, that's for certain.
Doors bang; clouds rush to the east.
So much disorder and the sky seems
bluer than ever, a page across which
indistinct messages are scrawled in haste.

So It Happens

The dark reaches up through a crack
in the horizon and drags the sun deep
into the night. That noise, is it an owl
perched in the bare branches of an oak?
What is that creature back on the path,
zigzagging forward, jittering its rags?
The night hot and damp like the inside
of a fist, or a tumor growing within him.
Not a real tumor, no. He tends it as one
might tend a garden. Grinding, grinding—
the turning of the earth on its axis.
This man loves the gun, that one the lily:
so each creates his idea of the world.

Tinsel

There were dreams in which he fell in love. The woman was no one from the real world. At times they touched, at times the touching was a promise that lay ahead. At times there were obstacles—distances to be crossed, moments to be found. At times it was easy from the start: the ecstatic tension, the joy in beholding the face of the other. And there, in the midst of sleep, he felt he'd soon be released from futility and disconnection. Then, on waking, he was crushed by his loss. This figment adorning his dream, it was dreadful to think she didn't exist, had never existed. For a few nights he hoped to dream of her again and instead came his usual dreams of searching for something among dark streets and cul-de-sacs. And if until then his life had seemed complete, now he felt a lack; if his life had been lacking, now it seemed empty. That's how it can happen in dreams—the intrusion of a tinseled deceit on which to base all hopes that turns the day to shadow.

Future

The skeleton of a horse, still noble
in a museum in Indiana, a century dead
and its service for the North long over;

or a stuffed St. Bernard in a monastery
in the Alps, honored for the near frozen
it saved from the snow; or something

modest, a two-headed rabbit packed
in a jar—so those friends he had lost or
were dispersed, buried, given to science,

how much better to have them stuffed,
mounted, fixed in a museum: One reading
a good book as he strokes his mustache;

a girl laughing as she flips off a bottle cap.
A favorite place to walk at the start of day,
running his fingers over the glass cases, like

seeing friends who can give advice almost.
Then a chair where he'd sit in the evening,
reading the paper by a lamp, a little music,

no one speaking but companionable, the world's
ruckus shut out. Hard not to go more often,
harder each time to leave. These imaginings

that grow as he gets older on how the future
might work out: ambulance rejected, doctors
sent packing. Only others would call it death.

Parable: Poetry

It was hot. At night the penguin dreamt of the Antarctic.
That's how it began. He bought a fan; he bought
ice cubes. He bought an old Ford convertible and let
the wind riffle his feathers. He rushed all over town.

It's my duty to be happy, he told himself. His life
took on new meaning. He hung yellow rubber dice
from the mirror, tied a raccoon tail to the antenna.
He sang along to country on the radio. He waved

at pretty girls. But soon his car began to cough,
as when a bit of steak goes down the wrong tube.
It shook all over like a kitten in winter. The vehicle
prepared to die. Luckily, a garage lay straight ahead.

The mechanic was busy, but said: Return in an hour
and I'll know better. So the penguin strolled to a diner
just next door where he ordered apple pie à la mode.
By far his favorite. Then he hurried back to the garage.

The mechanic was stretched out beneath the hood,
his face smeared with grease. Engine parts lay
scattered across the floor. You got real problems,
said the mechanic. Your fuel pump's busted,

your generator's shot, your carburetor's rusted
and it looks like you've blown a seal. Nah, said
the other, wiping a drop from his bill, It's ice cream.
Freeze this moment. The penguin wore a benign

and self-satisfied expression. The mechanic's
expression showed confusion and rising distaste.
Then bit by bit the two swapped how they looked.
The penguin showed hesitation and the mechanic

had the critical demeanor of a man ready to correct
the other. Isn't this how it is with poetry? Both
had examined a creation with multiple meanings
as mystery moved from perplexity to possibility

to discovery. The mechanic with neither patience
nor learning again showed disgust; the penguin
revealed revelation. Where would we be without
language? The perception of one and confusion

of the other could easily be expressed in a sonnet.
Sad to say the mechanic hated poetry. As for the penguin,
stuck to his brain with the nail of surprise was a sense
of the human condition, which let him see himself

afresh, and only arose after he'd worked to attain
a modicum of meaning. Didn't this explain his silly grin?
As for the mechanic, his brain was blank, apart from
intense revulsion: an emotion that lessened his chance

for a humanistic vision. He didn't get that poetry
offers the opportunity to see the world through
a pristine lens; and maybe, just maybe, if he stared
hard enough, he might find himself staring back.

Scale

For Heather McHugh

In the stratification of domestic perception,
the man walks through the living room and notes
the mantel's pricey bric-a-brac; the child stares up
at a light bulb, brighter than the sun beneath
the floor lamp's shade. For the dog, it's knees
and tabletops. For the cat, it's the darting escapes
of the small. Mouse, cockroach, and louse—worlds
scaled to discriminating ambitions and dimensions.
How easily overthrown when the man, in his hurry,
stops and turns, puts a hand to his heart, and then
drops past mantel, lamp, and tabletop—thump!

Now his eyes focus on the coffee table's claw foot,
next on a single polished claw stretched toward
a scrap of walnut hung up on filaments of carpet,
a tidbit dropped by a grandson. After that, he spots
specks of lint, dust motes that grow with his attention
so huge they change into solar systems with planets
where he might see cities, rooftops and, who knows,
even a man mowing his lawn, if he had the time.
But now his eyes fix on a vortex of pink spirals, ridges
and rills whirling inward to the labyrinth's still center
where at last his focus stops. Why, look, it's his own
dear fingerprint. First there forever, and then not.

Cut Loose

Perhaps this is what death is like
when the soul first separates
from the body. He feels cut loose.

Trees extend in all directions,
gray columns to hold a cloudy day.
Was it like this for her? It might

have been like this. It's late fall;
dead leaves carpet the trail. Earlier,
when he entered the forest, red paint

marked the trees to show the way.
Then he saw fewer; now he finds none.
Cut loose from what? Cut loose

from the living. Birds squabble
among the leaves, sparrows or
chickadees; he can't tell which.

The wind has stopped. Should he
turn back? Who's to say what's back?
Who's to say he'll find the last tree

with its slash of red? What did it
look like? A tree, that's all, leafless,
like the others. Was it like this for her,

a constancy of gray? He wavers
between reason and invention.
It's mid-afternoon; the sun sets early.

Snowflakes seek out paths between
a latticework of branches. Which
way is forward? He's been offered

a collection of mistaken directions.
The silence, surely she experienced
a similar silence, its frigid palpability.

What was it like for her at the end
with the gray pressing in? He needs
to see what she might have seen,

to hear what she heard till he feels her
nearby. Snow collects about his boots;
deepening twilight, deepening cold.

Death must be something like this:
an absence within an absence. Cut loose
from what? Cut loose from the world.

He holds his breath to feel her close.
She is nowhere; she is empty space.
Damp fetor of decaying leaves.

Recognitions

The awful imbalance that occurs with age
when you suddenly see that more friends

have died, than remain alive. And at times
their memory seems so real that the latest

realization of a death can become a second,
smaller death. All those talks cut off in mid-

sentence. All those plans tossed in the trash.
What can you do but sit out on the porch

when evening comes? The day's last light
reddens the leaves of the copper beach.

Laugh

Hayden Carruth (1921–2008)

What he wished was to have his ashes flushed
down the ladies' room toilet of Syracuse City Hall,
which would so clog the pipes that the resulting
blast of glutinous broth would douse the place clean
much in the way that Heracles once flushed out
the Augean stables. After serious discussion,
his wife agreed to do the job. Such an action
was in keeping with his anarchist beginnings,
letting life come full circle and being his ultimate
say-so on the topic of individual liberty. Luckily,
or not, he then forgot, or wiser minds prevailed,
I don't know, and his ashes were packaged up
for the obligatory memorial service—probably
more than one—so the mayor and his council,
all the lackeys, flunkies, toadies, and stoolies
caught up in a shit-spotted cascade down those
marble steps and into the astonished street
is an event that exists first in my imagination
and now in yours. But I'd also have you see him
in those last days in his hospital bed in Utica's
St. Luke's, wearing the ignominious blue and
flower-specked nightie the nurses call a johnny,
stuck with more tubes than a furnace has pipes,
and contraptions to check every bodily function
including the force of his farts, while his last bit
of dignity was just enough to swell that fetid bag
hanging like a golden trophy at the foot of his bed.
Blind and half-paralyzed, a bloody gauze mitten
to keep his hand from yanking out his piss-pipe,
his skin hop-scotched with scabs and splotches,
his hair and beard like the tossed off cobwebs
of a schizophrenic spider, he listened, when

those of us in the room felt certain he had fallen
into his final coma, listened as his wife read a note
from a friend who wrote: How could death matter
since his prick had shuffled off its mortal coil
some years before? And he laughed, he burped out
a truncated snort, an enfeebled guffaw from fluid-
packed lungs, and those of us with him laughed
as well. Friends, to none will it come as a surprise
to say we're trudging toward the final dark
or that to each of us in life is given a limited
allowance of laughs. Save one, save one, to ring
death's doorbell and ease your final passage.

Acknowledgments

American Poetry Review: "Alien Skin," "Casserole," "Furniture," "Gardens," "Inexplicably," "Laugh," "Lizard," "Monochrome," "Never," "No Simple Thing," "Pain," "Prague," "Sincerity," "Skin," "Skyrocket," "Song," "Swap Shop," "Technology";

The Autumn House Anthology of Contemporary American Poetry, Third Edition: "Leaf Blowers," "Stars," "Wisdom";

Boston Review: "Parable: Horse";

Great River Review: "Fly," "The Miracle of Birth," "Wisdom";

Narrative Magazine: "Mrs. Brewster's Second Grade Class Picture";

New Letters: "Exercise," "Niagara Falls," "Persephone, Etc.," "Recognitions," "So It Happens," "Stories," "The Wide Variety," "Winter Wind";

The New Republic: "Scale";

The New Yorker: "Determination";

Normal School: "Stars," "Wisdom";

Ploughshares: "Crazy Times" (under the title "What You Should Have Thought About Earlier"), "Narrative";

Plume: "Melodrama," "Statistical Norm," "Water-Ski," "What Happened?";

The Plume Anthology of Poetry 2013: "The Dark Uncertainty";

Shadowgraph: "Jism," "Thanks," "Valencia";

Southern Indiana Review: "Future," "Leaf Blowers," "Turd";

Terminus: "Parable: Fan/Paranoia," "Parable: Gratitude," "Parable: Heaven," "Tinsel";

Union Station: "Good Days."

About the Author

Stephen Dobyns was born in Orange, New Jersey, and has lived in twelve states and in more than thirty towns and cities, as well as having lived for nearly four years in Santiago, Chile. With his new book, he will have published forty books: fourteen books of poetry, twenty-three novels, one book of short stories, and two books of essays on poetry. He has taught at about a dozen colleges and universities, but most consistently he has taught part-time with the MFA Program at Warren Wilson College, having begun in 1977 when the program was at Goddard College. He spent nearly two years working as a general assignment reporter for the *Detroit News* from 1969–71. From 1995 to 2007, he wrote about thirty feature stories for the *San Diego Reader*. His first book of poems, *Concurring Beasts*, was chosen as the Lamont Poetry Selection for 1971 by the Academy of American Poets. His fifth book, *Black Dog, Red Dog*, was a selection of the National Poetry Series (chosen by Robert Hass) in 1984. *Cemetery Nights* received the Melville Cain Award from the Poetry Society of America as the best book of poems published in 1986–87 (shared with Margaret Gibson). He has also had poems appear in the *Best American Poetry* series and has received *Pushcart Prizes*, as well as having received prizes from the *American Poetry Review*, *Poetry Magazine*, the *Virginia Quarterly Review*, and other magazines. He has received a fellowship from the Guggenheim Foundation and three awards from the National Foundation of the Arts. Two of his short stories appeared in *Best American Short Stories* and two received Pushcart Prizes. He has written many reviews and some articles for the *New York Times*, *Washington Post*, *Chicago Tribune*, *Philadelphia Inquirer*, *Times Literary Supplement*, and several literary magazines. He has three children and presently lives near the ocean in Westerly, Rhode Island.

BOA Editions, Ltd.
American Poets Continuum Series

Colophon

BOA Editions, Ltd., a not-for-profit publisher of poetry and other literary works, fosters readership and appreciation of contemporary literature. By identifying, cultivating, and publishing both new and established poets and selecting authors of unique literary talent, BOA brings high-quality literature to the public. Support for this effort comes from the sale of its publications, grant funding, and private donations.

The publication of this book is made possible, in part,
by the support of the following patrons:

Anonymous
Gwen & Gary Conners
Mary S. Mulligan Charitable Trust
Steven O. Russell & Phyllis Rifkin-Russell

and the kind sponsorship of the following individuals:

Anonymous x 2
Nin Andrews
Nickole Brown & Jessica Jacobs
Bernadette Catalana
Christopher & DeAnna Cebula
Anne C. Coon & Craig J. Zicari
Jere Fletcher
Michael Hall, *in memory of Lorna Hall*
Sandi Henschel, *in honor of Kevin "The Bold" Nolan*
Grant Holcomb
Christopher Kennedy & Mi Ditmar
X. J. & Dorothy M. Kennedy
Keetje Kuipers & Sarah Fritsch, *in memory of JoAnn Wood Graham*
Jack & Gail Langerak
Daniel M. Meyers, *in honor of James Shepard Skiff*
Deborah Ronnen & Sherman Levey
Sue S. Stewart, *in memory of Stephen L. Raymond*
Lynda & George Waldrep
Michael Waters & Mihaela Moscaliuc
Michael & Patricia Wilder